Ayurveda for Dogs

Dr. Vinod Verma

Ayurveda for Dogs

Health, healing and importance of dogs in the Vedic tradition

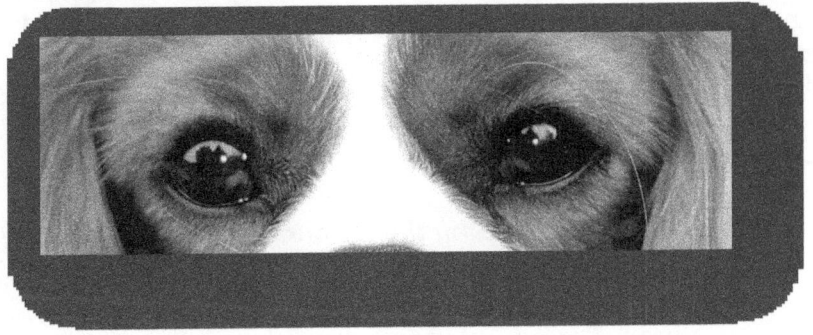

Gayatri Books International

The information provided in this book is not intended to replace the services of a veterinary physician. The book is written for the purpose of helping people to manage their pet better for a healthy long life. The author and the publisher are in no way responsible for any medical claims regarding the material presented in this book. For using recipes provided in this book at commercial level requires the prior permission from the author. For more information, write to the author directly.

Copyright © Dr. Vinod Verma 2013
Present edition is published by Gayatri Books International Himalayan Centre, Village Astal, Dunda, Uttarkashi-249151 Uttrakhanda, India

German edition: 2012 by Oertel+Spörer, Reutingen, Germany

The nutrition part of this book was separately published as 'Good Food for Dogs' in 2007.

All right reserved. No part of this book may be reproduced or transmitted in any form or by any means, mechanical or electronic including recording, photocopying or any information storage and retrieval system without the written permission from the author. Brief passages may be quoted by the reviewers and commentators.

Translation rights are held by the author. Write to her directly at ayurvedavv@yahoo.com or ayurvedavv@gmail.com

Visit Dr. Vinod Verma at www.ayurvedavv.com to find out about her other publications and other activities like seminars, lectures, consultations, etc. Look for more information on the last pages of the book.

Photographs and cover design by the author
Consultant: Mohit Joshi

ISBN: 978-81-89514-22-8

Dedicated to Brave Gopi,

who fought heroically with a Bhagera (leopard) on a snowy winter night and escaped from his claws with a hole in her head. I healed her and she lived healthy for 18 months. Unfortunately, some parasites remained in her blood, the wound reopened and she died at the age of three in our Himalayan home.

Preface

Ayurvedic principles of health and healing are applicable to humans, animals and plants equally. I have done extensive research on women's ailments and their Ayurvedic remedies. Traditionally, the same remedies are given to domestic cows and water buffalos as to women. To enhance milk in a nursing mother, we give *kalonji* (*Nigella sativa*), cumin, fenugreek, and cress seeds. Same substances are given to domestic cows and buffalos to enhance milk production. In case of loss of appetite, Ajwain (something like thyme) is given to these animals, just as it is given to the human beings. Like the human nutrition, the nutrition for domestic animals is according to season. The cows and buffalos themselves choose to eat specific grasses during certain season and that care is also taken in giving fodder to domestic animals. The dogs are never given foods which produce too much heat in their body and in summer, it is taken care that dogs are given cooling things like rice, wheat preparations and milk.

This book is based upon the age-old wisdom of Ayurveda. It includes general methods of care and psychology of dog, massage, nutrition and remedies for minor ailments. The communication with dogs is through touch and there is a description of Ayurvedic massage and herbal bath for dogs. The book lays an emphasis on healthy nourishment for dogs. Just like we eat warm and freshly prepared food for good health, dogs will be healthier if you share a part of your food with them. Dogs do not have a language like us to communicate and the poor animals cannot protest against the unhealthy, dried and stinking industrial food one gives them. Their protest, at the most, will be not to eat for a day or two. Dogs have a very strong appetite due to their high body temperature and they need to eat even if they dislike the food they get. I request all dog owners around the world to be sensitive to their dogs and puppies, understand their 'language' regarding their nutritional needs, their psychology and also learn to heal their minor troubles.

I have highlighted the importance of dog as a domestic animal since antiquity in the world and in the entire

Vedic tradition. Dog had a very high place in various cultures of the world due to its highly developed senses and its benefits to the humanity. That is all the more reason that we should treat this creature well and learn simple and practical ways for its health and healing through this book.

Ayurveda for Dogs

Sheru

Acknowledgements

I express my deep gratitude to Professor Dharmanand Sharma of Panjab University for making me aware of the importance of dog in ancient Indian culture and in the Vedic tradition. Many inspiring discussions with him opened my mind to various aspects of this fine animal in diverse civilisations of the world.

I am grateful to all the dogs from Germany and India who cooperated in my research. Special thanks go to Beau-Beau from Munich, Sheru from the Himalayas and Leon from Freiburg. With their loving and communicative ways, they always told me about their likes and dislikes. Thanks also to the wonderful Tuffy of the Nagars in neighbourhood in Noida for posing for massage pictures.

Ayurveda for Dogs

Beau Beau

Leon

'The six characteristics of a dog are: numerous teeth, satisfied with very little, deep sleep but very quickly alert from the sleep, devotion to his owner and gallantry.'

Chanakya

3rd century B.C.

Ayurveda for Dogs

Contents

	Preface	7
	Acknowledgement	11
	Citation	13
1	Ayurveda: the Science of Health and Healing for all Living Beings	17
2	Dog Psychology	31
3	Massage and Bath with Ayurvedic Products	45
4	Ayurvedic Nutrition in Context of Dog	55
5	Some Health Promoting Vegetarian Recipes	65
6	Healing Minor Ailments and Promoting Strength	83
7	Post-natal care of the Pet and the Puppies	101
8	Importance of Dog in Human Civilisation	107
	About the Author	*135*

Ayurveda for Dogs

1
Ayurveda: the Science of Health and Healing for all living beings

Ayurveda is the science of health and healing from ancient India and it is the mother of all medical sciences. It is holistic in the true sense of the word, as it is based upon the fundamental unity of the cosmos. Same principles apply to the cosmos as to all living beings of both plant and animal kingdom. The whole cosmos and everything that exists in the phenomenal world is made of five fundamental elements or mahabhuta, namely ether (space), air, fire, water and earth. These five elements form the material reality of the universe that also includes all living beings. The same principles apply to the body as to the rest of the cosmos. All what exist can be divided into two categories- jada and chetana. Jada is without consciousness and chetana is with consciousness and has a soul.

Living beings, whether they are humans or animals or plants are chetana. They have their biologically independent system and all the living processes are taken care of by their vital organisms. They have a part of the Cosmic Substance or Prakriti and another part of the universal Soul- Purusha. They are connected to the cosmos through prana or inhalation and exhalation of the vital air. For the performance of all physical, mental and organisational functions in a living being, the five elements take the form of three principal vital forces known as dosha, namely- vata, pitta and kapha. The principle of health lies in keeping the three vital forces (tridosha) in equilibrium so that they can perform their respective functions and are in harmony with each other. If they are not in equilibrium, the perfected system of a being is disturbed and there are ailments and malfunctions. The three vital forces in a living system are constantly influenced by external factors like nutrition, time, place, situations, mental state and behaviour.

As we observe each day, the five elements in the cosmos are dynamic and well coordinated and form a perfected system. The sun brings us warmth and light each day and the darkness of the night is beautified with stars and the changing phases of the moon. There are clouds, rain, snow, and the rivers are gushing towards their destination. From the dynamism of the five elements, seeds become sprouts; trees lose their leaves and get new ones. The living being from both plant and animal world die and new life comes to being.

Like the cosmos, an individual living system is also perfect and dynamic. It is a part of the cosmos and likewise it is constituted of the five fundamental elements. But the elements in a living system are present in the form of three energies or doshas in order to perform all the functions of this particular system. Let me explain to you briefly their individual functions.

The Three Principal Energies of the Living Beings (Tridosha)

The five elements give rise to three energies called the vata, pitta and kapha (tridosha) to perform all the functions of the living body.

Vata is constituted from elements ether and air and its functions are related to these two elements. Ether or space is omnipresent and air is mobile. The functions related to movements as well as to space are performed by vata.

> **Vata** is responsible for all movements, blood circulation, respiration, excretion, speech, sensations, touch, hearing, feelings like fear, anxiety, grief, enthusiasm etc., natural urges, formation of foetus, sexual act and retention.

Fire constitutes the pitta energy of the body and thus pitta is the living being's fire or agni. When we use the word agni in Ayurveda, it pertains to everything related to digestion and assimilation. Agni in Ayurvedic terminology is a part of pitta but pitta has also some other functions.

> **Pitta** is responsible for vision, hunger, thirst, digestion and assimilation of food, heat regulation, softness, lustre, cheerfulness, intellect and sexual vigour.

Kapha forms the solid part of a living being and is responsible for the formation of new cells. Living beings constantly need new cells. There is a formation of various secretions and juices.

> **Kapha** constitutes all the solid structure of the body and is responsible for binding different organs together. It gives rise to firmness and heaviness to the living system and is responsible for sexual potency, strength, forbearance and restraint.

Just as the equilibrium of five elements in the cosmos is important for an order and harmony in the cosmic system, similarly, for good health of a living being, a balance of these elements is needed. Dosha equilibrium should be maintained by living with the rhythm of nature. If we go against nature, eat too much or too little or too frequently or do not sleep during the night or sleep during the day and do not care to go to the toilet on time, and so on, our system is disturbed with these anti-natural acts. Animals are in tune with nature and when they feel unwell for some reason, they also know how to bring themselves back to health by natural means. However, when we impose our anti-natural ways of living on our pets, they feel unwell and their system is disturbed. For example, some people give food to their dogs too frequently and too much. There are others who give their dogs whatever is leftover and dog ends up eating too much. There are still others who give their dog strictly industrial diet. The industrial diets cause imbalance in the body. If we eat dried and canned food all the time, we get constipation, too much thirst and restlessness. Similarly, the dogs get all these symptoms and feel unwell.

Individual Variations

Living beings differ from one another because of a slight difference in their fundamental constitution called prakriti in Ayurveda. This difference is due to the variation in the proportion of the three main energies. Prakriti not only describes the variations in physiological features of individual living beings but also their personality types. The fundamental constitution of a being is a very important theme for basic understanding, nutrition and maintaining health.

Ayurveda: the Science of Health and Healing

Ayurveda places a great emphasis on basic constitution or prakriti, which can be seen from a living being's appearance and behaviour. Prakriti is due to the dominance of one or two doshas in a living system. Besides the physiological reactions of living beings, prakriti also determines the basic behaviour.

Nature has provided all living beings the intuitive quality to live in coordination with space and time (desha and kala). Cows or other grazing animals choose specific grasses during different seasons to maintain balance during hot or cold weather. Living beings also chose food according to their age and specific circumstances to maintain their fundamental constitution or prakriti. If out of greed or force, too much or wrong foods are taken or other deeds are done which are against the principles of nature, the living beings become unwell and feel physically uncomfortable. This is the diversion from the state of prakriti or the fundamental constitution to vikriti or a state of imbalance. In the state of vikriti, the living body tries to heal itself and reverts back to prakriti. We all have also an intuitive wisdom of doing the right thing to help nature and heal ourselves. Animals and humans living close to nature have still this wisdom, while those living remote from nature in the cities have mostly lost it. Diet and living style should be according to age, time of the day, time of the year, weather, season, geographical location and particular circumstances.

If the living beings ignore the state of vikriti and do not live according to time and space, it takes the form of an ailment (vyadhi). With nutrition and other simple external measures, one can attain the state of vikriti to prakriti and thus, not only one regains physical well being, also these methods are used to treat problems like anger, irritation, impulsive behaviour, and so on, which are due to vikriti at mental level.

PRAKRITI ⟷ VIKRITI

Prakriti or the fundamental constitution of the living beings denotes the natural variations. Just like our appearance differ from each other and no two human beings are exactly alike, similarly, our inner being has variations. You can recognise your dog amongst hundreds of other dogs. Similarly, there are actions and reactions of the living being which are variable to different degrees.

Prakriti

According to Ayurveda, each living being has an individual constitution from birth. It is the basis of the physiological and psychological reactions in beings.

The prakriti of an individual is due to the dominance of one or more energy and attributes the individual the characteristics of that particular dosha in slightly more predominance than the others. For example, the pitta prakriti individuals are sensitive to heat, sweat a lot and eat and drink in plenty. The vata prakriti ones are agile and swift in their movements. The kapha prakriti persons are slow and stable in their movements and are more tolerant than the previous two. In the mixed prakriti, the person may experience different attributes at different times and in different situations.

Seven types of prakriti

VATA   VATA-PITTA   SAMADOSHA (all energies in equal proportions)
PITTA   PITTA-KAPHA
KAPHA   VATA-KAPHA

Prakriti or the fundamental constitution in living beings is their basic personality. Some react faster than others and are agile. This is the domination of vata or a being is said to have vata constitution or prakriti. Vata prakriti beings have vastness of space and rapidity of the wind that constitute this energy. There are others who are exactly opposite, are slow to react and these ones are with the heaviness of earth and water and have kapha constitution or prakriti. There are others who are more dynamic than these two and are clear and decisive in their actions. These are the ones with pitta prakriti. In the mixed prakriti, there are variable reactions depending upon the dominance of a particular dosha according to circumstances, situations and time. Further, the degree of the domination in each type of prakriti and the proportion of the two dosha in the mixed prakriti leads to innumerable variations in living beings.

Whether it is for your children, pet or other members of the family, it is essential that you learn to accept the individual variations and do not expect the same reactions from every one. Do not compare your dog with other dogs condemning that yours react slower than that of your friend's. The problem comes only when your otherwise slow dog is still more slow or sleeps more than normal. That means, the pet is suffering from kapha vikriti. Similarly, when your agile dog reacts nervously, the pet has vata vikriti. Skin irritation and rash, red eyes indicate pitta vikriti. Observing these signs of vikriti are important in the present context, as you will be able to treat your dog with specific food to heal its vikriti.

If the vikriti or the state of being unwell is left unattended, it takes the form of a disease or an ailment over a period of time. Thus, dealing with vikriti, there and then, is the greatest of prevention from ailments. State of vikriti also gives rise to fatigue and lowers the immunity of the body. Thus, the prolonged state of vikriti makes the living beings vulnerable to disorders caused due to external attacks of virus, bacteria, parasites, etc.

This is a brief introduction of the fundamental principles of Ayurveda. I would like to add here that the dog has a very high place in the Vedic tradition due to its highly developed senses. Dogs have the same five senses as we humans do, but as mentioned above, three are more developed than the human beings, whereas the sense of taste is deficient. Olfactory centre in dog is immensely developed and the sense of smell is immeasurably better than that of humans. Shepherds and Blood Hounds have an even better developed sense of smell than the other dogs and are used for tracing missing persons, toxic substances, drugs, explosives, etc.

Dogs' sense of taste is poorly developed as compared to humans. However, due to their highly developed olfactory senses, they decide to eat or not to eat by smelling the food.

Dogs possess an acute sense of hearing. Dogs are able to register sounds of 35,000 vibrations per second compared with 20,000 in humans. They are also capable of shutting their inner ear in order to filter the distracting sounds.

Dogs have very well developed long distance vision whereas their short distance vision is poor. They are also capable of seeing in poor light. In fact, dogs can see better in poor light whereas in strong light, their vision is blurred.

In the Vedic tradition, which is followed until present times, the dog is one of the three important animals to get offerings to the dead forefathers, the other two being cow and crow. Dog is called Shvan in Rigveda and it has many synonyms in Sanskrit (see the last chapter). The dog was considered as one who prevents hindrances in achieving a goal. Later on, in the Brahmanas, it is said that the horse and the dog are the most important companions for travelling. The dog provided direction and the horse lent speed in the history of civilization and allowed human beings to be able to expand on the globe. Dogs are depicted symbolically as helping death in the Vedic tradition.

Ayurveda for Dogs

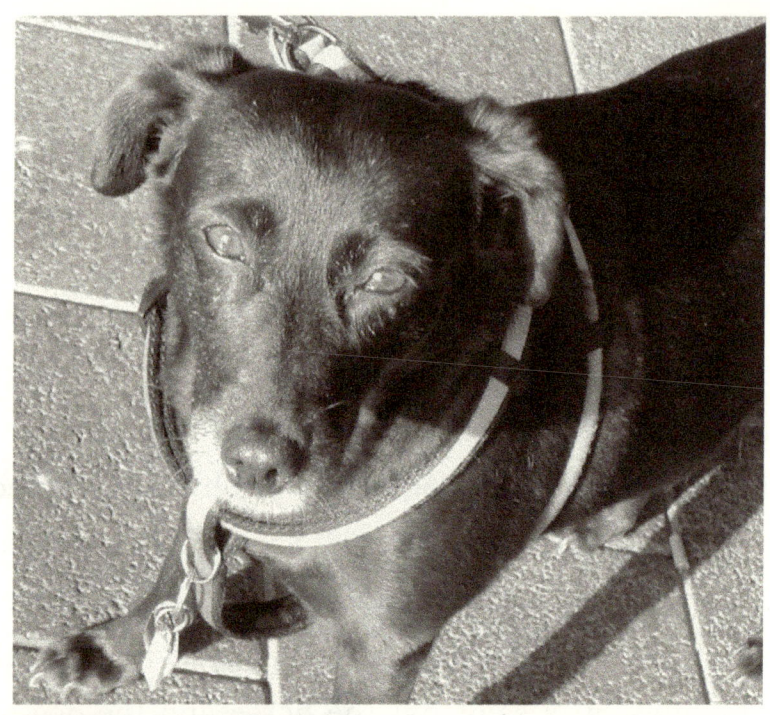

2
Dog Psychology

Domesticated dogs have been adapted to live with human beings and are conditioned that way. Dogs by nature live in company of other dogs or humans. Although they are adapted to live with human beings and as part of the family, the studies show that dogs raised without any human contact retain their inherent instinct and prefer relationships with other dogs over associations with human beings.

Dogs are very communicative animals and show their instinctive emotions of love, gratefulness, demands, etc. through various gestures. Their communication with their master is through their expressive eyes, mouth and tongue and some varieties greet members of the family by wagging their tails. They love to be touched and caressed.

There are always great stories told and shown in the films about the charismas of dogs and their loyalty to their masters. Like the variations in human beings, dogs also differ from each other for being sincere, honest and loyal. Their intelligence levels also vary regarding their task performance or their ability to respond to the training for specific tasks. One should be cautious about the information provided in some books or films where dogs are shown as intuitive, emotional and super-communicative animals. This kind of data is on a small sample of exclusive animals ignoring a large majority of dumb and stupid dogs. It is like if we write on the lives and achievements of some great scientist, musicians, artists, etc. and try to depict the whole human race on that basis. According to my direct experience (which is of course limited), there are certain breeds of dogs which have an inbuilt discipline and ability. Once somebody brought me a puppy in my village in the Himalayas. The person told me that it was a mixed breed between Himalayan Shepherd and some normal street dog. The Shepherd father of this puppy was also not a pure breed. It was very hard to train this little one and he cried all the time. At this point, an expert dog breeder from the high Himalayas came to me with a beautiful pure breed shepherd puppy. This puppy was only one month old and the previous one was three months.

However, this one was easier to train and even at this young age, he was very conscious of his own cleanliness and his excreta. The dog breeder told me that it is a waste of effort trying to train the previous one, as their inherent learning capacity is very low. He showed me how to look for a good dog from the shape of their ears and paws.

According to the Vedic tradition, just like in human beings, the inherent ability in dogs is also karmic. The inherent wisdom from birth is the result of the karma in the previous lives. Since it is a very profound and extensive theme, I will not get into detail in the present book, which is meant to be a practical guide. Nevertheless, I would like to mention that several dog lovers have told me the stories when they felt a special connection with a particular dog in their lives and they could not forget that specific dog all their lives. There are others who told me that they found a particular dog 'saintly'. I myself had a very exclusive experience with Sheru- the Himalayan Shepherd in our Himalayan home. Generally, before I was preparing to part from the house, Sheru was quite indifferent to me. He was generally hiding somewhere instead of accompanying me to the door of the farm. It was like he was upset about my departure and did not want to show his emotions. But once, while I was departing, Sheru sat down on the step of the main entrance to the house and blocked my way. I really got irritated, as there was a 12 hours drive ahead of me. It is only later that I realised why he did that. I had forgotten a bag with all the telephones and other important papers inside the house. I realised that only after having driven about 50 Kms and wished I had better understood the symbolic gesture of my wonderful dog beforehand.

There are the subtle and profound aspects of a being which are intricate in both, humans and animals. In the next section, I will explain the basic behavioural personality based upon Ayurvedic wisdom which will help you to understand your pet better.

Understanding your Pet and his Prakriti

As is said in the previous chapter, the Ayurvedic wisdom highlights the individual variations in all living beings. Even the siblings can be extremely diverse in nature given the fact that they are born to the same parents and are brought up in more or less similar circumstances. Therefore, do not compare your dog to the previous dog or to other dogs in the neighbourhood. First of all, the dogs of different prakriti or the fundamental constitution have different behaviour. Do not find your kapha prakriti dog lazy and passive. These are more stable, sincere and affectionate. Despite that, they are quite adept in being aloof and do not give much trouble being left alone in the apartment. On the contrary, your vata prakriti dog may be rapid to react but troubles you by jumping on the guests. You get problem when you have guests who do not like to be touched by dogs. Pitta prakriti are generally quiet but get very angry if they are teased in one way or the other. They can even bite when angry.

Changing Behaviour with Vikriti

You have to take care of your dog's behavioural personality and understand it. Your dog may at times behave strangely and unusually due to vikriti of a particular dosha. For example, if a dog, who has already vata prakriti is fed on the dried commercial food, it gives rise to vata vikriti and that makes this being nervous, hectic and unmanageable. This food gives rise to dried throat and the dog is always thirsty despite drinking water. The symptoms are more enhanced in dry and windy weather. Similarly, a kapha prakriti dog gets into kapha vikriti due to canned and cold food. It may feel lazy, excessively drowsy and have too much of salivation.

However, this does not mean that only a vata prakriti dog can have vata vikriti or a kapha prakriti can have kapha vikriti. Simply, with a particular prakriti, they are more vulnerable to get that vikriti.

Knowing the prakriti of your pet is important, as that will not only help you to understand the behaviour of your pet, but will also be helpful in healing him. For example, if you have a dog, who is agile and swift and is quick to react to your gestures and commands, this pet has vata prakriti. Due to the effect of windy weather or some dried foods, you may observe that your dog is uneasy and nervous. The pet's nervous behaviour is due to vata vikriti. To bring him back to normal, you have to learn to heal his vikriti, which can be easily done by making some semolina halva for him. Recipe for this is provided in the later part of the book. Thus, with such a simple way, you can heal your dog and also save yourself of his restlessness. By the way, if you yourself have the same symptoms of restlessness, the remedy is the same. The whole cosmos works on the same principles.

Vikriti is a diversion from the state of health, which is prakriti and it not only gives us physical discomfort but also psychological uneasiness. When we make personal efforts to retrieve our state back to prakriti, we revert back to a psychological comfort zone.

If you find that your pet is unusually barking at the passer-bys or is getting agitated with nothing much, it is the sign of pitta vikriti. It is normal that the dogs get this vikriti in summer. Those varieties are more vulnerable which are from cooler climates and are made to live in relatively warm weather. It is easy to treat this with food and drink. Add some milk (10 to 20%) in the water you give to your pet and give him some well-cooked rice with a pinch of butter in it. Alternatively, you could also add some milk in the cooked rice. Please do not give any readymade food like milk rice bought from a store. Those contain sugar and preservatives. Dogs get immediately skin irritations due to sugar and they may get vata imbalance due to preservatives.

If your dog has kapha prakriti, you will observe that he usually has an easygoing nature, is habitually obedient and loves to sleep. However, the dark rainy days of winter or some heavy to digest or fatty food may cause kapha vikriti. You may observe that the pet sleeps more than usual and is slow and dull in his movements. He may have also too much saliva. Some spicy food and taking the pet for longer walks than usual will help treat the kapha vikriti. Please note that when I say spicy food, it does not mean chilly. One should not give chilly to the dogs as they have already high agni or the digestive fire. In case of kapha vikriti, one should add pepper, cumin, clove, cinnamon, etc. in small quantity in the food or use one of your own spice mixtures that you use in your food. You will find the details and recipes in the later part of the book. Here we are dealing principally with how the vikriti also influences the behavioural pattern of your dog and instead of getting irritated on your poor pet, you should be able to treat him with some simple methods.

Territorial Behaviour

Dogs are extremely territorial animals and will do all to defend their territory. The territory of the domesticated dogs is based on the limitations of their owners.

Male dogs mark their territorial boundaries by urinating or rubbing their scent on the ground or on trees to warn other animals of their presence. When they are on neutral grounds, which are not considered their home territory, they greet strange dogs by sniffing, tail wagging and posturing. Unless they want the same prey or are engaged in courting the same female, they usually go their own way after a brief interaction. Female dogs can be very aggressive to protect their young once. As soon as they smell other animals or human beings in the vicinity, they are already on the defensive and react aggressively. Be very careful with your female dog with puppies, as they are hypersensitive at this stage and can be hostile even to the owner.

The fundamental basis of the territorial and protective behaviour of the dogs is based upon their highly developed sense of smell, which is referred to as the divine sense in the Vedic scriptures. From choosing their food to self-protection and to guarding their young ones, the dog's sense of smell is a protective weapon with them. We recognise objects and living beings from their appearance, whereas the dogs do so by smelling them. Imagine you see a friend from a distance and you greet. Similarly, dogs know from quite a distance about objects and other dog's or another animal's specifications. We act and react to the objects and situations after visual information, whereas dogs do so by their olfactory sensation.

Behavioural Personality

Like human beings, the dogs have varied personalities and intelligence levels. However, there are certain behavioural patterns which can be assigned to breeds. They have enhanced characteristics according to the work they were bred to do. Sporting dogs are adventurous and will follow their noses wherever scents lead them. They respond enthusiastically to the calls from familiar humans. On the other hand, the hounds and watchdogs are more aloof and independent in nature and are not so much interested in human interaction. Working and herding dogs are businesslike in their disposition. They see the situation and act instantly. They are instinctively protective towards their herd.

Ayurveda for Dogs

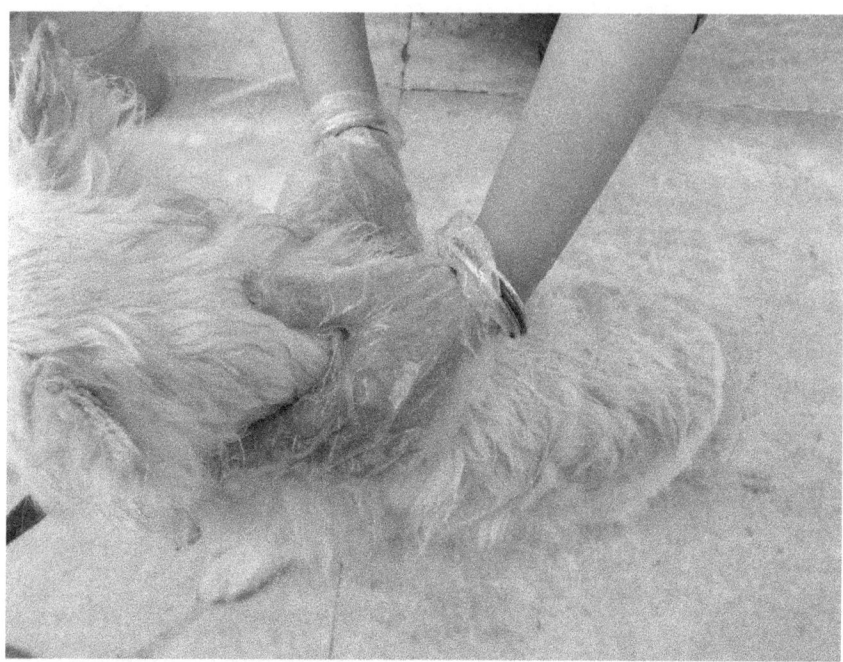

4.

Massage and Bath with Ayurvedic Products

Your dog does not have a language as you have. However, the dogs are very sensitive, affectionate and emotional animals. They understand the tonality of the language and they generally yearn for a touch of affection. The purpose of this chapter is to give your pet a comforting and healing touch. Besides that, there are some herbal treatments which will help your dog get hygienic skin and a healthy appearance. They help make the outer skin stronger and resistant to wounds.

Massage

Prakriti Variations

Dogs of different prakriti are variable to the extent of touch they like. The massage has to be oriented according to the prakriti of your dog.

The kapha prakriti dogs like to be touched frequently and for a long time. They can sit beside you calmly and while you massage them or simply stroke them, they generally fall asleep.

The vata prakriti dogs also like to be stroked and massaged but they do not sit calm for a long time. They are easily distracted with small things, noises or smells and move away.

The pitta prakriti dogs do not like to be touched too often. They need massage but for a short duration.

Massage and Bath with Ayurvedic Products

This is a brief description of variations of massage in dogs based on their prakriti. With this knowledge, you will begin to understand the diverse behaviour of your pets and will learn to act accordingly. It is also important to know that there are two more factors which one should keep in mind in this context. There are individual variations which depend upon the basic nature of the dog (karmic as has been explained earlier). Secondly dogs of different varieties also behave differently. For example, the watch dogs generally do not like to be touched much. They also take time to develop a relationship with you. A watch dog in a farm house or a normal home is like a member of the family but one should take into account the difference in its behaviour for touching, massage and bath, etc. One should not tag them as 'cold in nature' or indifferent to human touch. In fact, these dogs are quite subtle in communication and take time to relate to you. Therefore, one should just proceed by slow and short steps with them.

Techniques of Massage

Pressing Massage

Generally people stroke their pet simply at the back. It is a way of communicating with your dog. However, for massage you have to apply pressure with your fingertips and the strokes should be smooth. You have to specifically reach each and every part of the body.

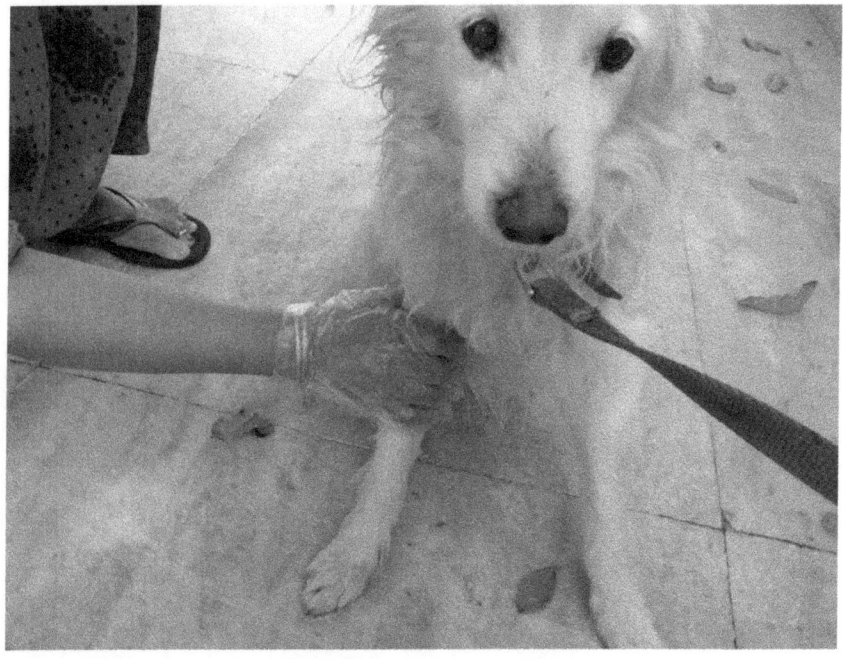

Begin from their paws by making small round movements and then upward to the leg by pressing lightly with your hand. When you have finished all the four legs, massage the sides with both your hands by putting light pressure with your fingertips. Do the middle of the back by pressing the backbone lightly between your three fingers and thumb. Lastly, put both your hands around the neck of your pet and stroke back and fourth. This is a very important part of the body as the circulation of the head region depends upon it and the nerve chord from brain passes through this narrow region for connecting the whole body to the brain.

Lepa (smearing) and Wet Massage

For humans, oil massage is highly recommended in Ayurveda. However, for dogs, it is not recommended, due to their high body temperature and also due to the presence of pelt. In Ayurveda, the wet massage is done with a series of products which are used for lepa or smearing. There are diverse products with different effects. For dogs, we principally use cooling products and disinfecting products.

Cooling Products: I will describe here some cooling products which are easily available everywhere in the world.

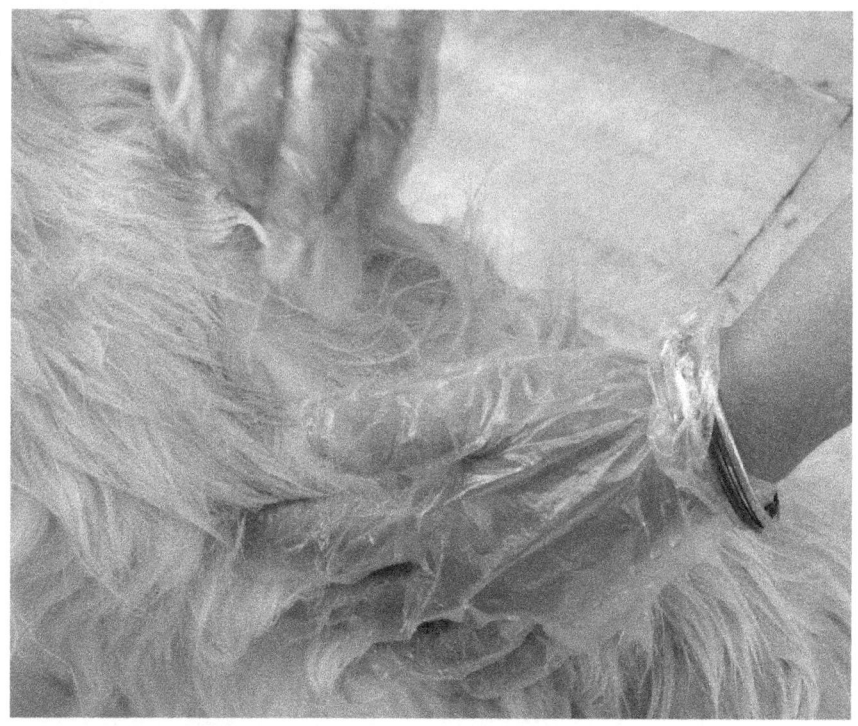

Healing earth: Unlike in human beings, where we apply a thick paste of healing earth on the body, for dogs due to their pelt, a thin paste is made. Dissolve three tablespoons in about two litres of water. Stir well to make it homogenous After putting this mixture everywhere on the body (not on the face) massage with your fingers as described above and then wash off the lepa by putting gradually warm water. Alternatively you can use a soft massage brush to massage while pouring the water to wash off the lepa.

Neutral Henna: This is specially recommended for imbalance of pitta and during summer months. Since henna has a colour, neutral henna that does not colour is available in the market. Soak three tablespoons of henna in some water over night to make a paste. Dissolving this paste in a litre of water. Apply like you did above and wash it off after a while.

Sandalwood water: Sandalwood dust is available at a reasonable price as compared to sandalwood oil and sandalwood pieces. Soak one tablespoon in about 500 ml water for a day and filter it. Smear all over your dog this perfumed water and leave it for a short while. Wash it off as described above.

Alternatively, few drops of etheric oils like jasmine, rose, etc. are used in about 500 ml of water to wet the dog and then the massage can be given with brush or hands.

Bath

Dogs do not need to be bathed as frequently as we human beings, but I will suggest that you make it once a week ritual to give your dog one of the massage treatments described above or do a lepa in summer and then bathe. It is better to clean the dog with soap before putting the perfumed lepas like sandalwood, jasmine, etc.

Bathing Soaps

As for human beings, for dogs also, I do not recommend body shampoos. They dry the skin and make it rough. This leads to skin irritations, vulnerability to infections and vata imbalance. As for humans, the best to bathe are the soaps of natural origin. For winter you may use soaps prepared with oils like olive oil or other oils. In summer, you may use the soap prepared with some colognes. The original Eau de Cologne company of Germany makes a wonderful soap that also disinfects the skin. Ayurvedic soap called Medimix is made with 18 different Ayurvedic herbs and is highly recommended. The use of such soaps keeps the insects away from your pet. If your dog has skin problems, do use this soap. It is available at Indian shops abroad. These days, it is easy to order products with Internet.

After making the dog wet, the soap cake should be rubbed gently. After that, give a light massage with your fingertips as described earlier so that the soap reaches under the fur. Wash it off with warm water while rubbing.

Disinfecting your Dog

There are various ways to disinfect your dog and that should be done from time to time.

Yoghurt Bath

If you feel that your dog has skin irritation and is trying to rub himself often against a tree, try giving him yoghurt bath. Take some active and organic yoghurt and add equal quantity of water in it. Mix well and apply as you did with the lepa. In this case, leave for about 15 minutes. Then wash it off properly while rubbing and massaging the body with your hands or a brush so that the smell of the yoghurt does not remain in the skin.

Aloe vera Bath

Aloe vera can be bought in crystal form. Take about 5 grams of this powdered crystal (one teaspoon); boil it in a litre of water for about 5 minutes. Filter it and smear the entire skin with this decoction. Pour gradually several times and rub it well with a massage brush. Take care that you leave the head region. The decoction is bitter.

4.
Ayurvedic Nutrition in context of Dog

Dogs have very strong digestive powers as compared to human beings. The digestive power is called *agni* in Ayurveda. Dog's liver is the largest internal organ of the body and has six lobes as compared to the two lobes of human liver. They can digest harder, heavier to digest foods as compared to the humans. Of course there are individual variations in human beings, as well as in dogs regarding the strength of agni or digestive fire. The body temperature of dogs is two degrees higher than humans and to maintain that temperature, they have higher metabolism and better capacity to digest.

As for the eating habits are concerned, the domesticated dogs have undergone the process of civilization with us. From the hunter cavemen eating raw meet, human beings have developed the fine culinary art and persons from the civilized world can no more digest the rough and raw food they ate thousands of years ago. Though, these animals still have the game instincts, but largely the domesticated dogs enjoy soft and well-prepared foods.

Dogs Choose their Food with their Noses

Although the dogs have a poorly developed sense of taste as compared to humans, but this however does not mean that they can eat almost anything without any distinction. Their sense of smell is highly developed and they choose their food by smelling.

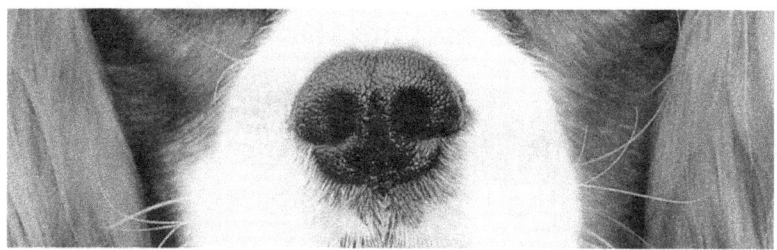

They never eat anything without smelling it first. In fact, with such highly developed olfactory centres, they can smell from far away and in such great finesse that we human beings cannot imagine. At times, we humans may put some offensive unknown things in our mouths and finding them awful, we spit them out. On the contrary, a dog will reject certain foods only after smelling them. I have never seen a dog spit out his food.

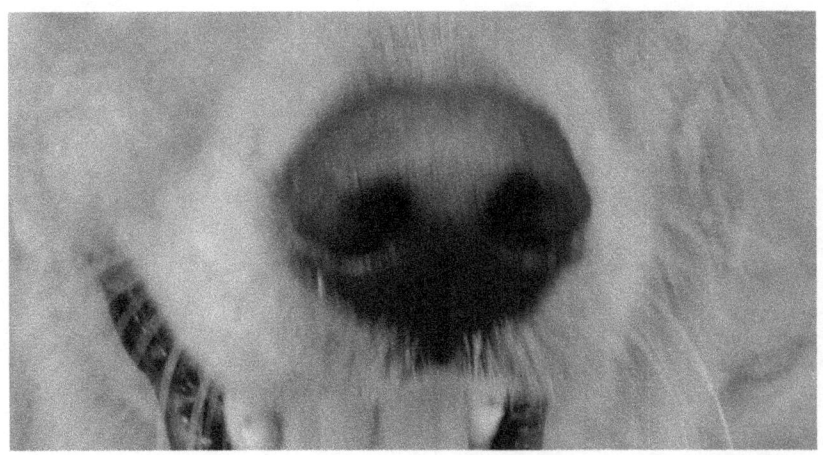

Many books on dogs say that dogs eat without distinctions owing to their poorly developed sense of taste and can almost live on the same food all their lives. I disagree with this view, as it seems to be the extension of human being's judgement from their own sense of taste.

When you are cooking a chicken or baking a cake or any other food which has buttery flavour, the dogs enjoy it and know exactly what you are making. They are looking forward to have it and I believe they are

Ayurveda for Dogs

very disappointed when they do not get to have any of these delicious items.

Different kinds of dogs vary in their food habits, but generally most dogs do not eat raw vegetables or fruits. Dogs are very fond of products of wheat, rice, maize and other cereals prepared with butter or milk. Dogs love dairy products.

Sensitivity to Dog's Nutritional Needs

Domestic dogs are like babies, both do not have a language to express their needs or register their protests. We have to develop sensitivity to their body language and learn to respond to their needs. When a baby cries or refuses milk, or lies listless, we get very anxious and make our best efforts to find out the problem. Similarly, dogs show their protests and tell you about the symptoms of their disorders in a symbolic manner. Sometimes, they love certain foods and if you give that repeatedly, they may protest after some days by not eating.

Observe always carefully the symptoms of any imbalance or vikriti. When a dog is not eating and is drinking a lot of water, he has an imbalance of vata (the ether and air energy). The vata energy is very dry. In such a situation, a warm semolina halva will be helpful. Similarly, in other situations like lack of appetite, vomiting or diarrhoea, one has to use food as medicine for dogs. This theme will be dealt later in the book.

Sweet things with sugar or honey should never we given to dogs. Although dogs like to have sweet biscuits and cakes, sugar is harmful for them and they get skin rashes with it.

Dog's Feeding Timings

Normally dogs should be fed twice a day— in the morning and late afternoon, and perhaps a few salty biscuits or nuts or something similar in between. The watchdogs keep awake at night and they need to be fed early morning and also later at noon. They should be fed in the evening, instead of late afternoon. Like the babies, dogs should be fed on time and in a regular manner. Their system gets oriented to those timings and they stay healthy.

As mentioned above, dogs have intense agni or digestive fire and are generally always demanding food. Part of the problem is that in a family, at times, different members have different timings for taking their meals. Smells of our food preparations give dogs a very high appetite. It is more linked to the desire to eat than to real hunger. This problem is partially solved when we begin to give the same food to dogs as we eat. Owners give their dogs canned or dried foods which generally stink or smell like fodder. They eat that to fill their stomach. Despite no hunger, the dog's desire to eat is evoked with the flavour of your food. This causes confusion and if you also give the food you have cooked, your dog will be over-fed. Therefore, the simple solution for a healthy domestic dog is to feed him the same or similar food as you eat. However, if human beings themselves are not eating healthy food and they take products made of white flour, consume industrial food and eat fried stuff, neither the master nor the dog will be healthy.

Try not to get your pet used to eating again and again. This happens mostly when people give their dogs the leftovers or are overindulgent and feed the pet frequently. According to Ayurvedic principles, it is toxic for the body if one eats before the previous meal is digested. The same principle applies to the dogs. Observe people around you who eat too frequently. They are perpetually sick with stomach problems and get a bad skin as well. The stomach has to go through the whole process of digestion even if you eat a piece of chocolate. Therefore, neither you, nor your dog should eat in an undisciplined manner.

Balanced Nutrition

The concept of balanced nutrition for dogs is not different from humans and they also need all the cosmic elements in order to be healthy, energetic and to live long. It has already been mentioned that the holistic principles of Ayurveda for health and harmony are not different for animals than for human beings. Like for human beings, a variety of foodstuffs are suggested for dogs. Both humans and dogs can very well be vegetarians but the diet must include milk. According to Ayurveda, vegetarian meals include milk and its products. Milk is of great importance in Ayurveda. It is a wholesome food and there is a mention of 14 types of milk from different animals in ancient texts of Ayurveda, and it is not only used as nourishment but also as medicine.

As mentioned earlier, dogs have higher appetite than human beings and they are able to digest those nutrients which are hard to digest for human beings. Due to their higher agni, dogs are always asking for food but we have to discipline them so that they do not eat too frequently and also not in excessive quantities.

If dogs are fed on a diet which not only fills them but also satisfies them, they will be healthier and stronger (for S-factor in food, see my book *Losing Weight with Yoga and Ayurveda* for more details). From the holistic point of view, balance does not mean only in the mechanical sense of proteins, carbohydrates, fats, minerals and vitamins, etc. It also means the food that rejuvenates you, enhances your immunity and vitality (ojas) and is according to time and place. Dogs also need to build up their ojas so that they are not attacked by ailments, their bones are stronger and they can live longer.

Like human beings, dogs enjoy a large variety of foods with varied nutrients. However, Western scientists think that since dogs have less-developed sense of taste, they do not need or enjoy a variety of food and can live on the same kind of foods all their lives. I do not agree with this view, as dogs are very choosy about what they eat. Although their sense of taste is lesser developed as compared to the humans, but their strong sense of smell makes them gourmet.

As stated earlier, the dogs select their food with nose. Owners of pet dogs can verify how the dogs distinguish between various foods and their likes and dislikes. All those who have dogs have the common remarks about their pets: My dog loves this or he is not fond of this or that, or he likes this more than that, or he prefers a particular brand of food, and so on. I am referring to the domesticated pet dog, as there are many stray dogs in the world who will eat anything due to lack a food available to them.

5

Some Health-Promoting Vegetarian Recipes

The health conscious people around the world know that preserved foods are non-promoters of health and life while fresh and organically grown foods are promoters of life. Similarly refined foods do harm to the body while holistic foods enhance vitality. In brief, the same principles of nutrition are applicable for your dogs, and they are not 'just dogs', they are your pets and you should treat them like a member of your family.

> GENERAL PRECAUTIONS ABOUT DOG FOOD
> - Never give your dog dried food like dried bread or crackers. You can give these things to your dog but soak them in milk.
> - Never give your dog very cold (out of the refrigerator) or very hot food. Cold food imbalances their body's energies. With hot food,

they end up burning their tongue and may get blisters in their mouth. Because of their high agni, dogs can never wait once the food is in front of them. Give them mildly warm food in winter or at room temperature in summer.
- Never give too much salt to your dog. It is better to give rock salt than sea salt. I do not recommend giving iodised salt.
- Never give sugar in any form to your dog. Avoid giving sweet biscuits or cakes.
- Do not give the dog fried stuff or fat from animals. Stick to olive oil, sesame oil or ghee (clarified butter) in small quantities. From time to time give a teaspoon of pumpkin seed oil with dog's food as nutrition supplement. Margarine is bad for the liver and should never be given to the dogs or to humans.
- Do not feed the dog too frequently or keep giving him the leftovers of your food. If you have leftovers, store them in the refrigerator for dog's mealtime.
- Never disturb or touch or caress your dog while he is eating.

Some Health-Promoting Vegetarian Recipes

I am giving below recipes for dog-food, which is healthy for your pet and also makes you use your food leftovers. Financially, it is a less expensive way to feed your dog as compared to the commercial foods you buy for them. On the other hand, this kind of nourishment requires you to make little effort as compared to giving dried or canned food.

Recipes

Bread

Commercial bread is widely eaten in the world, especially in Europe. Most health conscious people buy whole-wheat or mixed corn bread or bread with all kinds of health promoting seeds and nuts. In the Arabic and some Asian countries bread is baked fresh everyday. In several Indian states, chapatti, the fresh whole wheat bread without any salt or fat, is made two to three times a day and eaten fresh. In most homes, there are always remains of bread. It is one of the cheapest staple food which is highly strength promoting. Dogs love bread. Out of the two major staple foods in the world, rice and wheat, wheat is more strength promoting and is needed especially for those who have lot of movements. As the dog by nature is a running animal, products of wheat are highly recommended.

Since bread is easily accessible as ready food, I will give below various combinations of bread as dog diet.

> Please take care not to feed your dog continuously with one single recipe described below. It is important to alter the recipes so that your pet gets right nutrition.

Traditionally, everywhere in the world, the bread is eaten with butter or some preparations of vegetables or meat which has some fat in it. Bread is also eaten with cheese or all kinds of bread pâté, vegetable, lentil preparations with oil (humus, dal, aubergine spread, and so on). Think of doing the same thing for your dog. Bread needs to be consumed with little fat. The fat acts as lubricant and makes it a wholesome food and easier to digest.

Some Health-Promoting Vegetarian Recipes

Bread and milk

Dogs love the combination of bread and milk. They like both these ingredients, given separately or together. Remember milk is a wholesome food. Always get full cream milk for your dog. Make small pieces of bread and pour slightly warm milk on them. Dogs generally drink the milk first and then eat the milk-soaked bread.

Whole wheat bread or four-grain bread or linseed bread or breads with various nuts are good for dogs as for human beings.

Bread with oil

Alternatively, give your pet bread with some olive or sesames oil on it. Both these oils are very good and they should be given to the dog in small amounts daily. The sesames oil has high contents of calcium and is good for bones. Alternatively, you may smear some butter in case you do not have oil, but avoid doing it too often. Clarified butter or ghee is certainly better for the dog than the butter. Please do not give your dog margarine, as it is not good for the liver.

Breads with Different Kinds of Soups

Do not forget to have an extra portion for your dog when you prepare a soup. Make small pieces of bread and pour mildly hot soup on it. The dogs prefer to have pureed soups. If you have vegetable pieces in your soup, some of the dogs may not eat them. They love dal soups (recipe is given later) and the vegetable soups which contain milk, cream or butter. Out of meat soups, chicken soup is the healthiest as it brings balance in the body. Do not give your dog soups made from commercial preparations like instant soups. Some soup recipes are described later.

Some Health-Promoting Vegetarian Recipes

Bread rolls

Dogs adore soft bread rolls. It is because of the flavour of yeast which is stronger than that of bread and the presence of small amount of sugar in them. However, do not give the rolls as main meal. You can treat your pet with these to replace a dog biscuit. Excess of yeast is not good either for you or for your dog.

Maize bread

It is very easy to make soft bread with maize. Weak and underweight dogs should be fed on this bread.

Ingredients for one meal for a medium sized dog:

Maize flour	100 g (½ cup)
Cumin seeds	¼ teaspoon
Ajwain	½ teaspoon
Salt	½ teaspoon
Cooking oil	2 teaspoons

Put all the ingredients, except oil, in a bowl, add water and make dough. The dough should not be hard. Mix the ingredients well and whip a little to make a homogenous mixture. Spread with a wooden spoon on a non-stick pre-heated flat pan (crepe pan) with little oil on it. Never put the dough on a cold or mildly hot pan. Cook it on low heat. Wait for about 5 minutes and then turn it around to cook from the other side. Add another teaspoon of oil. Wait for 3-4 minutes to cook this side. Let it cool down before giving it to your dog.

Breads from other grains with the above recipe
Mixed flour breads

Mix flours of black gram (called *besan*), wheat and buckwheat flours in equal portions and make the bread in the above-described manner.

Similarly, you can make combinations with other flours like millet, barley, wheat, etc.

Rice or bread with soups

Carrot-potato soup

Ingredients:

Carrots (medium sized)	4
Potatoes (medium sized)	1
Curcuma	1 teaspoon
Cumin powder	½ teaspoon
Salt	½ teaspoon
Milk or butter or ghee	small amount

Some Health-Promoting Vegetarian Recipes

It is a very healthy soup as carrots bring balance of the three energies in the body. Cut these vegetables and cook them in half litre water after adding spices and salt. When they get soft, puree them with a hand mixer or a blender. Add some cream or milk or butter into this soup. Give your dog this soup with pieces of bread soaked into it.

Dal soup

Dal is a general word for a variety of split beans. They are sold with or without husk. The ones without husk are quick to prepare and are easy to digest. According to Ayurveda, mung beans bring balance in the body. I describe below a mung dal soup. But you can prepare the same recipe with mung beans after soaking them in water for 24 hours. They are at the beginning of the process of germination and are strength promoting.

Ingredients for a day's meals for a medium-sized dog:

Mung dal	100 g
Curcuma	1 teaspoon
Cumin seeds	½ teaspoon
Fenugreek seeds	½ teaspoon
Fennel seeds	¼ teaspoon
Coriander	¼ teaspoon
Salt	½ teaspoon
Garlic	3 cloves
Ghee or olive or sesame oil	1 tablespoon

Soak the dal in water for 10 minutes after washing it. Add this to ½ litre boiling water containing spices and salt except garlic. Let it cook for 15-20 minutes on low fire or about 8 minutes in the pressure cooker. Add

Some Health-Promoting Vegetarian Recipes

garlic and oil in the end. Give your pet this dal soup with some rice or bread.

Mashed mixed vegetables with rice or bread

Take small portions of various vegetables and cook them with the same spices as described for the dal soup recipe. When they are soft, blend them. Add fat and garlic in the end. Give these to your dog either with cooked rice or with pieces of bread.

Baked preparations with cheese

When you make baked vegetable or pasta preparations with cheese, do not forget to leave a portion for your pet.

Cheese

You can give your dog small pieces of cheese from time to time along with some bread and some olive oil on the bread. Do not give ever more than 200 g of cheese in a week. Let us say that you give this meal with bread and cheese only twice a week. In any case, milk is preferable for the dog as compared to cheese.

Cheese produces heat in the body, whereas milk cools it down.

Sugarless cakes

When you bake a cake, remember to take the share of your dog from the cake's dough prior to adding sugar into it. Bake separately a little cake without sugar and treat your pet.

Some Health-Promoting Vegetarian Recipes

Salty cakes

Cake with a tiny amount of salt can be baked specially for the dog. Or if you happen to bake a fruit pie, make a little more dough and bake it separately without fruits for giving your dog a special treat.

Potato Puree with milk

Potato is good food for both dogs and babies. Many people in this world think that potato is an unhealthy food. This false impression is because of the French fries (*pomme frites*), which are extremely popular around the world and are unhealthy due to the excessive fat they contain.

Put potatoes in the boiling water with their skin on and cook them until they are soft. Peel and mash them well and add a tiny bit of salt. Add milk to make them semi liquid. Mix well and give to the dog mildly warm.

Peanuts and other nuts

Dogs love to eat nuts and you can feed them on various kinds of nuts. Peanuts are fairly cheap everywhere in the world. You can also use other nuts. But do not use the nuts in excess. They should be in

Some Health-Promoting Vegetarian Recipes

addition to their staple food like bread or rice. They make the diet balanced by adding proteins and fat contents to the other foods described above. Do not give more than 50 to 80 g per day depending on the size of the dog.

Germinated gram (brown chickpeas)

Gram or brown chickpeas are like normal chickpeas but they are smaller in size and darker in colour. They are strength-promoting grains. The gram flour (*besan*) has been mentioned above to make bread. For an optimum food value, soak them in water for 24 hours. They get soft and can be given to the dog as such without cooking. The germinated brown chickpeas have great therapeutic value. 50 to 100 gms are given to people suffering from constipation, headaches or migraines. They should be taken every morning empty stomach for about 15 days or until cured.

These can be given as an in between snack or accompanying some other food during the main meal. For example, if you are giving bread and milk to the dog, give these first. If you give the dog bread and milk before, they may not eat the chickpeas later. To give the gram as a main meal, they have to be cooked and I give a recipe below.

Chickpeas

Brown chickpeas

You can use normal chickpeas also. Soak them in water a little longer than the brown variety. However, brown are more strength-promoting and keep the body's energy in balance.

Some Health-Promoting Vegetarian Recipes

You can also make an alternative recipe from germinated gram. Boil them along with potatoes for about ½ hour or 10 minutes in the pressure cooker with some salt and curcuma. Mash the preparation a little with hand mixer. Add a tablespoon of olive oil in the end. The whole thing becomes like a thick soup.

For a day's meal for a medium sized dog, you need 150 gm of gram and 3 medium sized potatoes.

Semolina Halwa

Ingredients for one day's food for a medium-sized dog:

Semolina	150 g
Ghee or butter	1 tablespoon

Roast semolina in ghee or butter on a low fire. After two-three minutes, add some water into it by stirring constantly. Semolina absorbs lot of water. You may need to add up to two glasses of water. Add as much water to make a semisolid preparation. In fact, it solidifies after getting cooled down.

Semolina with milk

Ingredients for one day's food for a medium-sized dog:

Semolina	150 g
Milk	200 ml

This recipe is very quick and easy to make. Add semolina into 250 ml of boiling water. Stir for about five minutes and then add the milk into it and cook for another minute.

Dogs love this preparation.

Dalia preparation with milk

Dalia is roasted and partially ground wheat. It is an Indian name. In Turkey, it is called bulgur. It is available in both Indian and Turkish shops in abroad. Ingredients for one day's food for a medium-sized dog:

Dalia	100 g
Milk	200 ml
Ghee	1 tablespoon
Fennel seeds	½ teaspoon

Roast dalia in hot ghee for about five minutes and add fennel seeds. Add half a glass of water and stir for 2-3 minutes. The grains will immediately soak water. Add milk and let it cook for another 5 to 10 minutes. Stir from time to time.

6
Healing Minor Ailments and Promoting Strength

Like human beings, dogs also get health troubles from time to time. If we take care and give them appropriate diet with special herbs and spices, we can restore them back to health. We can also give our dogs some health-promoting things with their diet so that they can develop a stronger immune system and can be saved from ailments.

Dogs are sometimes ill with problems related to liver. As has been said in the earlier part of the book, they have six lobes of liver and it is the largest internal organ of their body. From the Ayurvedic point of view, they have higher agni or power to digest and have more heat in their body as compared to human beings. Following are few reasons for dogs to get minor ailments related to liver:

Ayurveda for Dogs

Healing Minor Ailments and Promoting Strength

- If you do not take care and keep giving food to your dog too frequently, their liver weakens after a certain age.
- When domestic dogs are outside the house, they many times eat whatever comes in their way. Dogs who have free excess to open space like the domestic dogs in farm houses or watch dogs or shepherds, they tend to kill and eat birds or rats or other small animals. If these animals are infected or sick, the dogs also get sick from their meat.
- The canned or dried food gradually disturbs the inherent balance of five elements in the dog and the imbalance over a long period of time make them weak and shorten their lifespan. The dried food imbalances vata (the space and air energy in the body). It dries up the dog internally and gives too much thirst. You will observe that the dogs on preserved food have to drink a lot of water after eating. Vata energy is also responsible for the functions of nerves and when disturbed, it makes the animal nervous and restless. Due

to this disturbance, the dog also goes through the phases of loss of appetite.
- The canned food generally weakens the liver and disturbs the pitta or the fire energy of the dog. Depending upon the quality, if too many fat contents are there in this food, the poor animal gets a sluggish liver as well as lethargic behaviour (disturbance of kapha or the water and earth energy).

Purification and Rejuvenation of the Digestive System

If you have been giving canned or dried foods to your dog, before switching on to Ayurvedic diet, purify and rejuvenate your dog's body in order to enhance his immunity.

Give the following diets for two weeks and then start giving your dog the rejuvenating oil described below with his Ayurvedic food for a month. During this time, give the dog some rice recipes along with Ajwain and garden cress seeds. Ajwain rejuvenates the liver functions and garden cress seeds are great blood purifier.

The **dose** of cress and ajwain depends upon the size of your dog. It varies between 1/3 teaspoon each of these two ingredients to ¾ teaspoon for big dogs for the whole day. You should make one of the following recipes everyday and add these seeds. The seeds should be cooked with food, otherwise dogs would not eat them.

The dog is not getting any milk during this two-week diet plan. To replace the animal fat, the pet should be given ghee (clarified butter) or butter as fat or olive oil.

Purification Diet Plan

Feed your dog for two weeks on one of the following recipes everyday. You can prepare one recipe each day and give the pet twice a day the same. This diet will purify dog's blood and rejuvenate the liver functions.

Khichari

Khichari is made with the combination of mung dal (split mung beans without husk) and rice. Take one portion of dal and two portions of rice. Soak them in water for 15 minutes after washing them. For a medium sized dog, you may need 75 and 150 g of dal and rice respectively for one day. Add these in 1 litre boiling water. Add 1 teaspoon of salt and a teaspoon of curcuma powder. Either cook in a pressure cooker for 10 minutes or on low fire with the lid on for about 30 minutes. At the end of the cooking period, add ½ teaspoon each of ajwain and cress and one tablespoon of olive or sesames oil or butter. Alternate these three (oils or butter) each day.

Rice with carrot and potato soup

Cook rice as usual after washing and soaking them for 15 minutes and cooking for 10 minutes in water two times the volume of rice. Depending upon the size of the dog, 100 to 200 g rice will suffice for the day. Separately, cook 3-4 carrots and two potatoes with ½ teaspoon of curcuma, and ½ teaspoon each of cress seeds and ajwain. Add one tablespoon of olive or butter. Cook for 15 minutes or 5 minutes in the pressure cooker and blend it to make a purée. Give your pet this soup with rice.

Note: Always make sure that the rice is well cooked. Partially cooked rice can give your dog stomach-ache. I come across many times in the West that people either overcook rice or leave it partially cooked. The latter is not at all good either for humans or for animals.

Rice with pumpkin soup

As described above, do the same soup with pumpkin adding the same spices and give it with rice.

Rice with mixed vegetable purée

Use different kind of vegetables in this vegetable purée. Use some green vegetable, along with a carrot, a zucchini, a piece of pumpkin and a piece of cabbage. Do not use cauliflower, aubergine, and paprika, as they are relatively hard to digest. Cook the mixed vegetables in minimum amount of water. Use pressure cooker or cook them with the lid on after adding salt and curcuma. Purée them, add ajwain, cress and oil or butter in them as described in the earlier recipes. Mix the vegetable purée with rice to feed your pet.

Semolina preparation with vegetable purée

Semolina, like rice, is light to digest. It is easy to prepare. For a daily dose, you may need between 100 to 200 g of semolina, depending upon the size of the dog. It is best to measure semolina like you measure rice for cooking. It is simple to add water in proportion to the volume.

Heat one tablespoon of olive or butter/ghee in a pot and add salt, curcuma, ajwain and cress seeds. Add semolina and stir everything together for about three minutes. Add three times the volume of water than semolina. Keep stirring and you will see that semolina absorbs all the water and the preparation becomes semi-solid. You can feed the dog with this preparation as it is. But for better nourishment, I suggest that you give it with vegetable purée (the recipe is described above).

Dalia or bulgur with green peas

It has been already described about Dalia in the diet plan.

Roast about 100 g (150 g for big dogs) of Dalia in one tablespoon of ghee. After roasting for five minutes on low heat, add a teaspoon of cumin, ½ teaspoon each of ajwain and cress seeds, 2 teaspoons of sesames seeds and ¾ teaspoon of salt. Stir and add three times water than the quantity of dalia. Add 50 to 100 g of green peas. Stir well and let everything cook on low heat and with the lid on for about 15 minutes or until all the water is soaked.

There are six recipes described above and you can alternate them according to your convenience and availability of products. Keep your pet on this diet for 15 days. You may use one of these recipes once a week as a precautionary measure for your dog's health. Reference to some of these recipes is made in relation to the minor ailments described later in this Chapter.

Rejuvenating Oil

This oil is for enhancing immunity and strengthening muscles and bones of your dog.

Ingredients:

Sesame or olive oil	1 litre
Rejuvenating products:	
Fennel	10 g
Cress seeds	10 g
Ajwain	10 g
Coriander seeds	10 g
Nutmeg	5 g
Cinnamon	5 g
Cardamom	5 g
Clove	5 g
Garlic cloves	15

Grind all these ingredients except garlic into fine powder. A coffee grinder can very well grind these spices. However, it is suggested that you keep a separate grinder for the spices in order not to mix the flavours. Peel and dry the garlic cloves for half a day. Add the powdered spices and garlic into the oil and shake well. Let it soak for a few days while you shake the bottle or container once or twice a day.

You can use one tablespoon of this oil with food recipes daily.

Healing Minor Ailments and Promoting Strength

Suggestion: I suggest that you make both olive and sesame oils and give them alternatively. These two oils are the best out of all the oils for you, as well as for your pet. Never give your dog any kind of refined oil or mixed vegetable oil or something similar.

Diet recommendation for minor ailments

When your pet becomes victim to some minor ailments, do not rush to give him strong synthetic medication. You can bring your pet back to normal conditions with various diets.

Diarrhoea and Vomiting

Due to two principal reasons, body throws out something, either by way of stool or vomiting.

- The first reason is that a living being has eaten something which is against the nature of the living system and the system does not accept it and tries to get rid of it automatically. This is a good sign, as it is self-purification and getting rid of toxicity from the system. In this case, we normally do not need any medication and it is a self-regulatory mechanism. We need to take some precautions with diet to help nature in this process of purification.
- The second reason for throwing out or diarrhoea is due to some external infection. In this case, the attack is stronger and the immune system of the body fights back the attack of an external parasite like a virus or bacteria. In this case, we need something that enhances immune-system, as well as something in the food that diminishes the hyper motility of the intestines (in case of diarrhoea) and products that enhance body's digestive fire (in case of vomiting).

In either of the above cases, feed your pet only khichari or rice with carrot soup. Use ghee (clarified butter) during the ailment as it is soothing for the system and has healing qualities.

In case of diarrhoea: Use a mixture of powdered fennel seeds and nutmeg. Add this mixture into cooked food. Mix well and do not cook after adding these two ingredients. Their medicinal value reduces with heat. This mixture diminishes the intestinal motility.

Daily dose: Take fennel and nutmeg in a ratio of 4:1 and powder them. The daily dose for the pet is between ½ to 1 teaspoon of this powder depending upon the size of your dog. Give this 2-3 times a day with their Khichari or rice.

In case of vomiting: Add a mixture of ajwain and powdered ginger in the diet along with some fresh lime or lemon juice. Add these at the end of cooking.

Daily dose: Take ajwain and powdered ginger in equal quantity. The daily dose is between ½ to 1 teaspoon of this powder depending upon the size of your dog. Add 1 to 2 teaspoons of fresh lime or lemon juice in each meal along with this powder.

Loss of Appetite

In case of loss of appetite, we have to enhance the digestive fire or agni of the pet. Give him the same diet as described above for vomiting.

Excessive Heat

In summer, many dogs feel uncomfortable, as they get excessive heat in their bodies. They become restless, itchy and get excessively thirsty. They also lose their appetite.

For treating excessive heat, give your dog the following diets more often:

1. Milk bread or other recipes with milk as described earlier.
2. Do not give your pet any oil. Give only ghee, as oils are hot in properties and ghee is cooling.
3. Khichari with a spoon of cooling mixture with each meal. The cooling mixture consists of a powder of fennel and coriander seeds in equal quantity.
4. Rice with a spoon of ghee without any salt or spice.
5. Give your pet the Dalia preparation with milk as described earlier.

Nervousness

In case you find your dog nervous and restless, take the following precautions.

- Feed your pet more with milk and milk products.
- Give him mildly warm food. Make sure the food is liquid with either vegetable or dal soup or milk.

Healing Minor Ailments and Promoting Strength

- To treat the nervousness, give 1/8 of powdered nutmeg each day. The best way to give it is to add a pinch of this powder in the soup.
- Semolina halva with little more ghee helps treat the nervousness.

Ayurveda for Dogs

A baby Boxer aged three months participating in a football game

7
Post-natal care of the Pet and the Puppies

Dogs are sexually matured between the age of six months and one year. But they are not socially matured until the age of two. The heat cycle of the female lasts between 18 to 21 days. The first stage is called proestrus. It begins with mild swelling of the vulva and a bloody discharge. It lasts for about a week. During this stage, the bitch may attract males but she is not ready to be bred and will reject all advances. The next stage is estrus when the discharges decreases and become pink coloured. The vulva becomes very large and soft and the bitch becomes receptive to the male. This stage may last for about 11 days. The third stage is the diestrus, when after a red discharge, the vulva returns to its normal size and the bitch no longer accept the male for mating.

The gestation period is 63 days. The number of puppies is variable from 2 to 10 depending on small or large breeds.

Care of the Pet

The process of giving birth causes weakness, and you need to take good care of your dog during this period with nourishing diet, which is vata balancing and strength promoting. You should give your pet halva, soups, and vegetables as described above. Heat some ghee or butter, add ¼ teaspoon of cumin and ajwain each in it and add to the soup or rice by roasting them a little. Cumin is milk promoting and ajwain takes care

Post-natal care of the Pet and the Puppies

of the digestive functions and for healthy milk for puppies.

Add some basil leaves in the milk and cook it a little. Give this milk with whole wheat bread to your pet. Basil enhances the immune system.

Give only soft foods like halva, rice, vegetable soup and bread with milk for the first few days. Give only butter or ghee during this time. On the fourth or fifth day, add the strength promoting oil (described above) into the diet. But keep up with extra cumin and ajwain in the diet so that there is enough milk for the puppies.

In case the pet does not have enough milk for the puppies, you should give twice a day half teaspoon of dill seeds. It is better to make powder of this seeds and mix this powder with pet's favorite food. It can be mixed with Vegetables or soups or even halva. If you are used to baking bread at home, you can add the dill seeds into it. In brief, the dill seeds should be given in such a manner that the dog does not reject them. As I said earlier, dogs are like babies and one should find various ways to give them health promoting and healing foods.

The pet does not like to be disturbed too much at this stage. With the fatigue of the birth and responsibility of the young ones, she may acquire temporarily an irritable behaviour. It is better to leave her alone and undisturbed with the puppies.

Diet for Puppies

Here are some diet recipes for puppies:

Make sure that the puppies have at least two weeks of nourishment from his mother. Otherwise they will always have a weak immune system.

Puppies are fragile and vulnerable like our newborn babies. We have to take due care with their diet and hygiene. Pay attention to the following for their nourishment:

- For the **first two weeks**, give exclusively cow's milk. The milk should be boiled after adding water 1/3 of its volume and a few basil leaves or cardamom or both of these. Give the puppy 100 ml of this every four hours. Even if the mother nourishes, you

Post-natal care of the Pet and the Puppies

do need to give some extra diet as due to several offspring, the milk may not suffice.
- During the **third week,** reduce the quantity of milk into half and at alternate times make dalia with milk as described above. But do not give the grains. Make thin preparation of dalia by adding a little more milk and water and give the thick starchy fluid from the top to the pet.
- By the **fourth week,** you can begin to give the entire dalia and also rice with milk to the puppy.
- From the **fifth to eighth week**, begin to give vegetable soups and rice and small quantity of bread with milk or vegetable soups as described above for adult dogs.
- Puppies may get diarrhoea from time to time. Add fennel powder into their food preparation to treat it.
- In case the diarrhoea is more, make a cold decoction with fennel. Fennel is sensitive to heat and therefore the decoction is not made by boiling it into water. To preserve the medicinal qualities of the fennel, put a

soupspoon of powdered fennel in 100 ml of hot water and let it lie for few hours. Add 2 teaspoons of it in 100 ml of drinking water each time.

- If the puppy vomits, give ajwain tea. Add one teaspoon of ajwain in 100 ml of boiling water and cook for five minutes. Filter and dilute it with another 100 ml of water and give 3-4 tablespoons every four hours.

8

Importance of Dog in Human Civilization

Dog is the most important domestic animal in the West, and also it is an important pet amongst the wealthy people of the rest of the world. Despite that, it has negative association in European languages. It has also many negative connotations in modern Indian languages, even though there is nothing of this kind in Sanskrit language and literature or in ancient scriptures. On the contrary, I will narrate some amazing stories from the ancient epics of India and importance of dog in rituals which are still there since antiquity.

Dog and pig are used in medical research as both these animals have physiological and anatomical resemblance to human heart (poor ill fated animals!).

Let us now see the importance of dog in diverse situations— in life or death, in language or research, in history or day-to-day life.

Have a Heart for your Dog!

Ones I was a part of a research team for developing a drug for heart surgery. We had a very able heart surgeon performing the heart surgery on dog after using this particular drug every week. My job was to take the biopsy before and after the operation to see if there were any morphological changes occurring in the cells of the heart ventricle after the use of the drug. Most of the time, the animal died after two days or maximum three days of the operation. After about six operations, I asked our honourable surgeon that if dogs died in a short period after the operation, how could we risk using this drug on humans. The reply was totally astonishing and amusing. "You are mistaken Dr. Verma, human heart is much tougher than that of dog's. Heart surgery has lost many years due to lack of this knowledge."

So dear friends, treat your dog nicely and tenderly as dogs have delicate and vulnerable hearts as compared to ours.

Importance of Dog in Linguistics

Negatively or positively, in life or death, in food or in shame– the dog is an important animal. Here are a few things I found in European languages. However, my knowledge is only limited to three European languages and I would welcome from the reader their findings in other languages.

English

English language is very rich in dog-related proverbs and similes. I have taken only a part of the dog-related proverbs and sayings. There are many more also in colloquial English.

- Sea dog (light near horizon portending storm)
- Dog's life (a life of misery or miserable subservience)
- Dog's death (die miserably or shamefully)
- Dog in the manger (a person who selfishly withholds from others something useless to himself. This comes from the fable of the

dog who prevented an ox from eating hay which he did not want himself)

- Dog in a blanket (jam pudding)
- Dog's nose (mixed drink of beer and gin)
- Dog's sleep (light and fitful sleep)
- Dog-tired (extremely tired)
- To dog some one (follow closely or to pursue someone)
- Dogged (obstinate, tenacious, persistent person)
- Dogfight (competition and quarrel)
- Every dog has his days (someone having nice time but it is thought by others that he/she did not merit it)
- Go to the dog (get lost)
- Going to the dogs (ruined)
- Throw it to the dogs (let it go, forget about it)
- Not a dog's chance (not the slightest chance)
- Take hair of dog that bit you (drink more to cure the alcohol hangover)
- Help lame dog over stile (to be a friend in need)

- Raining cats and dogs (heavy rain)
- Let the sleeping dog lie (not to talk about some past misunderstanding or hostility)
- Love me, love my dog (accept my friends as yours)

French

- Temps de chien (bad weather).
- Avoir du chien (to get the elegance and seduction of a woman).
- Coiffee à la chien (to get a hairstyle with the falling hair on the forehead).
- Entre chien et loup (end of the day and beginning of the night).
- Etre chien avec quelque'un (to be hard on someone).
- Recevoir quelqu'un comme un chien dans le jeu de quilles (to receive someone very badly).
- Rompre les chiens (interrupt a conversation which has a dangerous subject).
- Se coucher en chien de fusil (to lie down with the bent legs).
- Vie de chien (miserable life).
- Vivre comme chien et chat (live life stupidly).

Ayurveda for Dogs

German

- Hunde arbeit (an awful job, devil's own job)
- Hunde elend (lousy)
- Hunde müde (extremely tired)
- Hunde gehen (to go to the dogs)
- Hunde wetter (foul or filthy weather)
- Hundsgemein (shabby, mean)
- Er kann hundsgemein werden (he can be really nasty)
- Es tut hundsgemein weh (hurts like hell)
- Hundsmiserabel (abominable)
- Hunde die bellen beißen nicht (Barking dogs never bite or empty vessels make most noise).
- Ein hunde von Mensch (a giant of a man)
- Hunde narr (masculine) (fanatical dog lover)

Ayurveda for Dogs

Sanskrit

In Sanskrit, the nomenclature of animal and plant kingdom designates their characteristic qualities. There are numerous synonyms for each plant and animal, and each reveals different characteristics and qualities of that particular creature or plant.

The name shvan, is first mentioned in the Rig Veda and it is a popular name until today. Shvan-nidra or sleep like dog is considered as good quality and healthy. The dog sleeps sound but wakes up at a slightest noise. In Hitopadesh, amongst the five signs of a good student, one is shvan nidra or sleep like dog. The other four are: effort like a crow, concentration like a crane, light nutrition and good behaviour.

Sanskrit Names for Dog and their Meanings

- Shvan: One with lower back
- Kukkurah: The one who makes noise seeing others
- Sarameyah: Sarama's son (story is related to the origin of the dog)

- Shunah: One who wanders here and there
- Kauleyakah: Born in a clan (of Sarama)
- Bhashakah: One who speaks (barks) a lot
- Mrigdanshakah: The one who bites others animals
- Vinash: Hunting dog
- Vishavkadru: One who is used for hunting
- Mrigari: Enemy of the wolf
- Alarka: This name is used to describe a mad or sick dog

There are still more synonyms is Sanskrit from various other sources. There is also a detailed classification of dog breeds, their nature in terms of description of their appearance and personality, as well as their caste written by Bhojaraja in *Yukti Kalptaru*. It is written in this book that a king should always have a dog for hunting, for knowing good and bad omens and for entertainment. The detailed description of dogs in the Sanskrit literature will be the subject of another book.

In Sanskrit, there are no negative connotations associated with dog as they are in English and other European language. In literature, there are sometimes mild allusions of the dog being inauspicious in relation to food or ceremonies. However, in modern times, there are many negative connotations with dog in the spoken language. It is abusive to call some one dog or a bitch. It is cursed by saying, 'may you die a dog's death'. It seems that the negative allusions came to the country later with the foreign invaders.

It is a pity that in the present times we give negative attributes to the dog and use it for cursing. Dog was so much venerated in ancient India that to call somebody as dog is not a curse but adoration. It is obvious that with such highly developed senses as compared to human beings, dogs are 'super' and are worthy of respect and a higher status.

Dog in Cosmogony

It is important to know about the story of Sarama, who started the clan of dogs. It relates more to cosmogony. Sarama was the bitch of Lord Indra, the god of heaven. She is considered as having divine qualities. The word Sarama means–the one with great attraction and beauty. Sarama helped Indra to discover cow and the infinite nutritional possibilities the cow has through its milk. It is written in the Rig Veda that Sarama discovered the path in the difficult mountains, took Indra there, heard the sound of the cow and followed the path further. Finally, she, along with Indra obtained the cow for the source of nutrition through milk.

Dog in Astronomy

In English, German and French and perhaps in other European languages as well, Sirius and Procycon are called Greater Dog and Lesser Dog.

Dog in the Vedic Tradition

In the Vedic pantheon, there are numerous gods and goddesses which represent diverse dimensions of cosmos in apparent and subtle manner. In this big cosmic family, animals are also included. I give you below some examples to illustrate the importance of dogs.

Importance of Dog in Human Civilization

Dog– the vehicle of god Bhairava: Gods always have a vehicle. The dog is the vehicle of god Bhairava. God Bhairava is the most destructive aspect of Lord Shiva. Destruction symbolises the cycle of creation and destruction like birth and death, spring and autumn, etc.

Dog watching the path of the dead: The god of death is Yama who owns two dogs with wide nostrils and four eyes. They watch the path of the dead. In my opinion, four eyes and wide nostrils signify dog's extra power of these two senses and that is why they are employed by Yama to watch the path of the dead. The significance is that dead persons arrive to Yama and do not divert back from their path to go back to earth. The dead persons leave their bodies but carry the burden of their karma on the soul. The accountability of good or bad karma is done in Yama's court.

God Bhairava with other gods, seen on the right side in the middle. He is accompanied by his dog.

Importance of Dog in Human Civilization

God Bhairava with his dog

Dog demanded justice from Lord Rama: The great epic Ramayana is about the story of Rama who was an ideal king of Ayodhya. He made sure that everybody gets justice in his kingdom and he personally attended to people who wanted justice every morning. One morning, there was no human complainant but the guards found a dog standing there with a wound on his head. He was asked to come in. The dog told Rama that he was hit with a baton by a Brahmin without any fault of his. The Brahmin was called and asked to explain why he did so. He told that he was hungry and irritated and the dog just happened to come on his way, so he beat him. The Brahmin received his punishment.

Dog being taken to heaven: In the great epic Mahabharata, king Yudhishthira was representing dharma or righteousness. At the end of his life, he was taken to heaven. He was accompanied by his dog. The lord of heaven, Indra, told him that he couldn't enter heaven along with his dog. He should leave the dog outside to enter heaven's gate. But Yudhishthira declaired that if so, he would prefer not to go to heaven as he could not leave his dog alone. The creature had given him company in his lone journey to heaven after his death. The conversation went as far that the king agreed to accept hell instead of heaven and take his dog along. In the end, it turned out that in order to test Yudhishthira's righteousness, Lord Indra had himself accompanied him in the form of a dog. The king was successful in the test and was allowed to enter the gates of the heaven with great jubilance.

Death rituals: To remember one's dead forefathers, homage is paid to them once a year. In this ceremony, symbolic offerings of food and drinks are made for them (*pinda dana*). On the name of five cosmic elements, these offerings are made to the following five: cow, dog, crow, young unmarried girl and ants.

Dog in Ancient Greek Mythology

The Greek goddess Hecate was the goddess of crossroads. She ruled over the souls of dead and instructed the mortals in the art of magic. She was accompanied by two dogs. Her statues were placed on the crossroads. Once a month on new moon, she was offered food. She was used for oracles. Here also, we find an indirect link of death with dogs.

Dog in Ancient Civilizations of the East

Dogs in the ancient times were also used as a beast of burden and there is historical documentation of their being used in wars. I cite below from the famous historian A.L Basham, who notes in his work *The Wonder that was India*:

> **'Half-wild pariah dog was as common in early India as it is today and dogs were also used in hunting. In the hills (Himalayas), a special breed of large dog, perhaps resembling the modern Tibetan mastiff, was famous beyond the bounds of India. The Persian emperor Artaxerxes I (465 to 424 B.C.) is said by Herodotus to have exempted the inhabitants of four Babylonian villages from taxes in return for their breeding Indian dogs for war and hunting. These dogs were also in Egypt of Ptolemies. With the Zoroastrians, the dog was a sacred animal.'**[1]

In ancient Egypt, dogs were thought to possess godlike characteristics. Amongst royalty, dogs used to have their own attendants, outfitted with jewelled collars and were fed on exclusive diet.

---

[1] Basham, A. L., *The Wonder that was India*, 1967, Page 198, Fontana Books, London.

On the death of a ruler, his favourite dog was interred with him to protect him in his afterlife.

Dogs in Our Times

Dogs are an integral part of the police force in the world to detect narcotics and other criminal activities. They are used by the blind and the disabled for orientation. Dogs are increasingly used in the world for companionship, specially for children and lone persons. Needless to say that dogs perform the exquisite task to guard farmhouses, as well as homes. They save our crops and fruits from other animals. Their highly developed sensory perception informs the owner much in advance of any human or animal invader. Dogs are used in Indian cinema to do amazing tricks– saving a woman from a rapist, making a thief fall from a wall, uniting two lovers and to remove misunderstandings between fighting clans by some trick or the other.

In an effort to integrate dogs in the society, some groups in India have been doing quite amusing things. I give below the two important happenings about dogs during recent times in North India.

Dog Weddings in Jaipur: In Jaipur, dog-lovers organised dog weddings and various owners brought their dogs for this purpose. The organisers told that there were 25000 pet dogs in Jaipur– the ancient city of maharajas. The organisers wanted to do all the Vedic ceremonies for the dog weddings but the Pandits protested and said that it was an insult to the Vedic rituals, as dogs, unlike humans have no lifelong commitment with one partner. Finally, the organisers could not do the Vedic weddings but nevertheless some ceremonies were performed with nice clothes for the dogs and other romantic celebrations for the pairs. It was a party time for both dogs and their owners.

Dog Fancy-dress Competition in Delhi: Dog-lovers in Delhi organised a fancy-dress competition for dogs. Owners were supposed to bring their dogs in fancy-dress and there was a panel of judges who decided for the prizes. All this was accompanied by big stalls of dog shops, dog-breeders and companies which make dog food and equipments. It was like a dog *mela* (festival at a magnanimous scale).

A spiritual dog from Kamakhya temple in Gauhati (Assam): Located on the Kamakhya hill in Gauhati, the capital of the state of Assam, this temple is a great Tantric pilgrim centre in India. There lives an Aghori Sadhu near the temple who owns a five months old puppy with very special nutritional habits. Oranges are his most preferred food. As solid food, he eats only uncooked rice, cashew nuts and almonds. He does not eat anything which is cooked and that excludes all preparations made of grains like wheat, barley, lentils, etc. He eats no meat or fish or any non-vegetarian food. He eats some selective raw vegetables. This kind of regimen is like that of a yogi. In the context of Indian thinking, where we believe in the cyclic notion of time and rebirth, we will interpret it as a yogi reborn as a dog due to some past karma.

Let us Care for Dogs!

Unfortunately, there are too many uncared dogs in world, which are prone to disease and suffering. Since the dog has played an important part in the history of human civilization, we should be kind and protective to the animal and every society should take due care to keep the dogs disease-free and nourish the animals well.

In Europe many people abandon their pets when they do not need them anymore or have to leave the country for some reason.

Fortunately in Germany and in some other European countries, there is a strong movement for protection of dogs and other animals (Tierschutzbewegung). There are several organisations under this umbrella, which have animal homes (Tierschutzheim) to take care of the abandoned animals. These uncared animals are given to volunteer new owners. Many people do this kind gesture to take over these animals as pets.

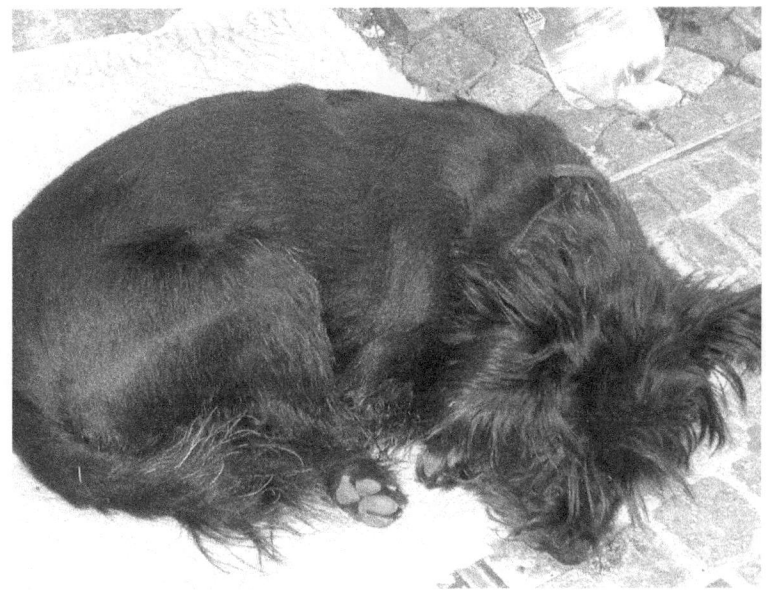

I end this book with the hope that the dog-lovers across the world can provide better care to their pets through the Ayurvedic knowledge provided in this book. The knowledge about the Vedic stories and the importance of dog in the world civilisation and cultural tradition can help regain the dog its lost honour and can lead the public to provide due respect and care to this wonderful animal. I also hope that this book will help to change the negative connotations about dogs and 'dog's life' will change.

About Dr. Verma

Along with a doctorate degree in reproduction biology in India, Dr. Verma studied Neurobiology in Paris University and obtained a second doctorate. She pursued advanced research at the National Institutes of Health, Bethesda (USA) and the Max-Planck Institute in Freiburg, Germany. At the peak of her career in medical research in a pharmaceutical company in Germany, she realised that the modern approach to health care is basically fragmented and non-holistic. Besides, we are directing all our efforts and resources to cure disease rather than maintaining health. In response, Dr. Verma founded The New Way Health Organisation (NOW) in 1986 to spread the message of holistic living, preventive methods for health care and to promote the use of mild medicine and various self-help therapeutic measures.

Dr. Verma grew up with a strong familial tradition of Ayurveda with a grandmother who had enormous Ayurvedic wisdom and was a gifted healer. She has studied Ayurveda in the traditional Guru-shishya style with Acharya Priya Vrat Sharma of the Benares Hindu University for 23 years.

Dr. Verma is an ardent researcher and is working hard to compile the living tradition of Ayurveda and spread it in the world through her books. She has published twenty two books on yoga, Ayurveda, Women and Companionship. The books are published in various languages of the world. Besides, she has published numerous scientific articles. Several other books are in preparation. She lectures extensively, teaches in Europe for several months a year, trains students at her two centres in India and gives radio and television programmes. A film on Ayurveda with her was made by German television in 1995 and was shown in 100 countries, in 130 languages. It was the first film on Ayurveda.

Dr. Verma has founded Charaka School of Ayurveda to train interested people with genuine Ayurvedic education so that they can further impart the knowledge of Ayurvedic way of life and save people from becoming a victim of charlatanry in Ayurveda. Dr. Verma is doing several research projects on medicinal plants and their combination in the form of remedies. She is the founder and chairperson of *The Ayurveda Health Organisation*, which is a charitable trust for distributing and promoting Ayurvedic remedies and yoga therapy in rural areas of India. She does regular lectures and workshops for school children in the rural and remote areas of the Himalayas to promote wisdom of traditional science and medicine. Dr. Verma gives seminars, lectures and teaches in the *Charaka School of Ayurveda* with guru-shishya tradition. She is the Academic Director of the *Charaka Ayurveda and Yoga Academy and Cultural Centre (CAYACC)*.

Dr. Vinod Verma's Publications

- *Patanjali's Yoga Sutra: A Scientific Exposition* (Published in English, Hindi and German).
- *Ayurveda for Inner Harmony: Nutrition, Sexual Energy and Healing* (Published in English, German, Italian, French, Romanian and Hindi).
- *Ayurveda a Way of Life* (Published in English, German, Italian, French, Spanish, Czech, Greek, Portuguese, Slovenian and Hindi).
- *The Kamasutra for Women* (Published in English [America and India], German, French, Dutch, Romanian, Italian, Portuguese, Slovenian Hindi and Malayalam).
- *Stress-free Work with Yoga and Ayurveda* (Published in German, English [America and India] and Hindi).
- *Patanjali and Ayurvedic Yoga* (Published in English, German and Hindi).
- *Programming Your Life with Ayurveda* (Published in German, French, English, Slovenian and Czech).
- *Ayurvedic Food Culture and Recipes* (Published in English, German and Hindi).
- *Yoga: A Natural Way of Being* (Published in English, German, French, Italian and Hindi).
- *Companionship and Sexuality (Based on Ayurveda and the Hindu tradition)* (Published in English and German).

- *Natural Glamour: The Ayurveda Beauty Book* (Published in German, Spanish, Slovenian and English)
- *Losing and Maintaining Weight with Ayurveda and Yoga* (Published in English and German).
- *The Timeless Wisdom of Ayurveda: A Scientific Exposition* (Published in English and German)
- *Prakriti and Pulse: The Two Mysteries of Ayurveda* (Published in German)
- *Good Food for Dogs: Vegetarian nourishment based on Ayurvedic wisdom* (Published in German and English)
- *Diet for Losing Weight* (published in German and English)
- *Aum: The Infinite Energy* (Published in German and English)
- *Pulse Diagnose in Chinese and Ayurvedic Medicine* (co-author for TCM Dr. Florian Ploberger) (published in German)
- *Shiva's Secrets for Health and Longevity* (published in German and English)
- *Healing Hands: The Ayurvedic Massage workbook* (published in English)
- *Prevention of Dementia* (published in German and English)
- *Ayurveda for Dogs* (published in German and English)

Himalayan Centre

Lectures, Seminars and Training Programmes

To get detailed information on the Charaka School of Ayurveda as well as our other programmes in India and Europe, visit our website or email us.

The New Way Health Organisation .NOW.
A-130, Sector 26, Noida 201301, U.P., India
Tel. 0091 (0)120 2527820 or (0) 9873704205 or (0)9412224820
Email: ayurvedavv@yahoo.com
Website: www.ayurvedavv.com

www.ingramcontent.com/pod-product-compliance
Lightning Source LLC
Chambersburg PA
CBHW020909090426

42736CB00008B/557